Body Language

The Art of Reading Non-verbal

Communication

Table of Contents

Introduction

I want to thank you and congratulate you for buying the book, "Body Language".

How this Book will help you:

This book contains proven steps and strategies on how to use the existing knowledge about body language to become better at reading others and expressing yourself. With this knowledge, you will be able to have heathier relationships, achieve your goals in the workplace, and influence people in the ways you wish to.

Many people wonder why the messages they try to get across never seem to get through, or why they can't seem to interpret those around them. A lot of problems with being understood and understanding others can be traced back to not knowing enough about body language.

Communication is about More than just Words:

Although we typically assume that humans communicate mostly using speech, body language is the most important factor in communication. This applies to personal relationships, professional environments, and even interactions with strangers. Body language is relevant to any situation that involves being seen or watching people communicate.

Communicating with others has a lot to do with listening. When it comes to body language in the observable sense, unspoken signals are constantly being traded whether words are being used or not.

This Type of Language is a Two-way Street:

What You Communicate: The body language you put forth shows what you truly mean and feel to those around you, whether you are aware of it or not.

What You Read from Others: The body language other people put forth will reveal their true meanings and feelings to you, if you know how to pay attention.

Receiving and sending messages using body language occurs on both subconscious and conscious levels. Another term for the study of non-verbal communication is kinesics, which comes from the word of Greek origin, kinesis, or "motion".

This type of communication involves feelings, thoughts, and intentions being expressed through physical motions, like eye movements, posture, the expressions of the face, hand gestures, and touch. This language exists not only for humans, but for animals as well. This type of language, unlike most others, doesn't have a grammar structure and is more open to interpretation than other languages, such as sign language.

In individual societies, there are interpretations that have been agreed upon for certain behaviors. These interpretations are not the same in each culture or country. Similar to this, there are questions as to whether body language is a universal fact or not. This language, related to general unspoken communication, serves as a complement to spoken words in interactions between people. It has actually been discovered by multiple studies that unspoken communication is responsible for most of the information exchanged during interactions between people.

Body language not only establishes relationships, or also determines the interaction between the two communicating. As important as this form of communication is, it can be rather unclear and ambiguous, which makes it important to learn how to interpret these signals accurately to avoid confusion or sending the wrong signals to others.

What Else is Involved in Body Language?

Personal Space: Body language also has to do with where one places their own body in relation to where others are positioned. For example, this could have to do with whether they place themselves in the middle of a room, very close to others, and whether they make themselves very small or spread out.

Small Movements: Body language encompasses motions that are almost imperceptible to the conscious mind, such as micro-expressions of the face and movements of the eyes. It can involve motions of the mouth or subtle eyebrow movements, as well.

Hand Gestures: The movements of a person's hands while they are speaking can say a lot about how they're feeling and even convey hidden messages in their speech. Hands are one of the major ways that the human species has developed to express itself.

Functions of the Body: Body language also covers areas that we wouldn't expect or even think much about typically, such as perspiration, breathing, blushing, blood-pressure levels, and even the rate of pulse. Although some of these are not perceivable to the naked eye, they can be intuited.

How does Learning how to read Body Language Help Us?

Words on their own, particularly when it comes to words related to feelings used in situations dealing with emotions, hardly ever fully reflect the true motives or meanings behind them. This means that looking for additional hints for interpretations is highly helpful to us. Reading body language will help you:

Know how those you speak with truly feel and what they mean. Often times, a person's tone or demeanor completely contradicts the words they are using.

To get a better understanding of how others may be interpreting our own unspoken signals and meanings, which we typically overlook.

To get a better understanding of ourselves beyond just the verbal communication we put forth to others.

As you can see by the list above, this is a subject that you can gain a lot from learning about, which makes this book a great place to start.

The trademarks that are used are without any consent, and the publication of the trademark is without permission or backing by the trademark owner. All trademarks and brands within this book are for clarifying purposes only and are the owned by the owners themselves, not affiliated with this document.

Chapter 1: The History and Background

Scientists and philosophers have seen the connection between physical behavior in humans with personality, mood, and meaning for many centuries, but body language has been a much more recent study. We have a long way to go with this sect of psychology, though it has become quite detailed and sophisticated when compared to older times. Recorded studies and research on this subject are either limited or non-existent until the middle of the twentieth century.

The First Thinkers to Consider the Subject:
The first experts we are aware of to contemplate this subject were the ancient inhabitants of Greece. Aristotle, Hippocrates had an interest in behavior and the personality of the individual. We can also assume that ancient Romans had an interest, and Cicero in particular, who enjoyed contemplating communication and feelings of humans. A lot of this interest in related subjects had to do with developing ideas about speech and oration, due to how significant this medium was for government and leadership in ancient times.

In more recent eras, written material on body language has appeared. We can look, for example, to the year 1605 at the works of Francis Bacon, where he reflected on the way gestures are an extension of verbal conversation. An author named John Bulwer published a book about hand gestures in the year 1644, and in 1806, Gilbert Austin explored the effectiveness of improving speech with gestures.

Experts on Body Language:
Darwin in the later part of the 19th century was the earliest influential academic figure to have observed body language in a serious and scientific manner. However, ideas in this area seem to have slowed down or possible halted altogether for the next century and a half.

The work of Charles Darwin opened the door to a lot of

ethological schools of thought, some of which started with studying the behavior of animals. In the early twentieth century, it was established, and then grew to cover the behavior of humans and the organization of social structures increasingly.

In the areas that ethology covers the evolution and communication of animals, the study strongly relates to the body language of humans. Ethologists have proceeded to apply the knowledge gleaned from these studies to body language, looking back the early origins of unspoken communication. Similar to psychology, ethology is a wide and varied science which continually clarifies our understanding of nonverbal communication and all it entails. The academic understanding of body language, in an accessible and popular format, is relatively new.

Julius Fast published a book on the subject in 1971 and commented that the science is so young that its experts are virtually unheard of. Fast was an award-winning author from America who published both non-fiction and fiction, focusing mainly on human behavior and physiology. His previously mentioned book was unique in that it was one of the first published works to introduce the subject of body language to wider audiences.

Although Fast was among the first, a few exceptions exist, such as Charles Darwin, who was a major influence to the author. Darwin published a book in 1872 which directly discussed emotions in animals and men. This work was among the first works published about the science of body language, even though it wasn't recognized that way until later on.

Early Psychologists Touching on the Topic:
In the later years of the 1800s, as well as the earlier parts of the 1900s, others would contemplate aspects of body language, such as Freud and other academics in the psychology field. These experts had an awareness of body language aspects such as personal space, but hardly ever focused directly on unspoken communication or came up with their own theories about the concept of body language. At the time, psychologists (including

Freud) were focusing on analysis for therapeutic reasons and behavior studies, much of which didn't see body language studies as necessary.

A book called The Naked Ape came out in 1967, published by Desmond Morris, which covered new visions of human behavior studies and touched on body language topics. The author was a zoologist from Britain and was fond of writing about human behavior and the way we communicate to the animalistic side of human evolution. The work of this author is still popular today, though slightly controversial, and can shed a lot of light on the way humans behave.

Even though Desmond Morris' books didn't directly mention or strongly focus on human body language, how well-received the author was had a lot to do with people's interest in the subject increasing. For the first time, widespread interest in body language had stretched beyond the scientific community and people were becoming more curious about the way we communicate with one another beyond words.

Facial expressions are arguably one of the most important aspects of body language, but it's difficult to trace scientific studies done on it in early times. However, some information exists on the topic.

Body Language Definitions:

Physiognomy: This is a related and quite obscure definition in the study of body language. The word describes expressions and facial features which have been considered to indicate an individual's ethnic origins, nature, or general character qualities.

The old roots of this word show that, although the idea of body language as a concept is a newly defined method of analyzing psychology, the concept of inferring character and the nature of an individual from expressions of the face is no new idea.

Proxemics: Earlier we briefly touched on the idea of personal space. Proxemics has been used as the technical definition to describe this concept. This word has been around since the mid-

1900s and was developed by an anthropologist using the word for nearness or closeness; proximity.

Kinesics: This term is used to describe the interpreting of communication using the motions of the body. This can refer to any behavior that is unspoken, uses movements of body parts or the full body, gestures, or facial expressions.

Chapter 2: How can we Use this Knowledge?

The concept of body language is a powerful idea that is understood by all successful and intelligent people. This can include you, as well. The theory and studies of this subject have come into the popular mainstream in recent decades because psychology academics have figured out what we mean to say with our nonverbal gestures. Our expressions and even the tiniest movements can all lend a clue to what we are feeling inside, even when our words don't convey it.

Nonverbal communication and body language are basically interchangeable concepts. Some consider body language to be only gestures or body positioning, while others consider it more in-depth than that. It is up to you to determine which area is most valuable to focus on, and thinking or studying the topic a bit should give you the answers you need for your own personal journey with the subject. By narrowing your focus on only the most relevant sectors of body language, you can hone in on useful information more effectively and become a self-made expert, eventually.

Here are some Questions about Body Language to Ponder when seeking to Understand the Topic:

Are eye movements and facial expressions included in body language?

Are perspiration and breathing involved in this language?

Since pitch and tone of voice are technically verbal actions, do you consider these to be a part of body language, as well?

The point of asking yourself these questions is not to find an objective answer, but to decide on what you find worthy of focusing on for your own personal discovery of what body language means to you. Another good reason to explore these questions is for the purpose of widening the scope of what body language means, in order to get the most out of meaningful signals in communication. These signals could be lost if they are not pondered and included.

It is easy to become confused when context and definitions are not clearly established. To take an example, many people commonly quote that unspoken communication makes up over 90% of what people take away from any given human interaction. Others state that such a generalization is impossible to make. The research that this quote is based upon actually focused on interactions that had a strong element of emotions or "feelings" to them. In addition, the estimation of over 90% included the intonation of vocal notes, which some don't consider to be an official part of the definition of what body language truly is.

What can be Agreed Upon with Body Language:

Regardless of failure from experts to agree on exact numbers or statistics on the topic, we can safely assume that body language makes up a large portion of what is expressed and interpreted in interpersonal communications. A lot of experts and sources of study appear to agree that at least half, and even up to 80%, of all interactions between humans are not verbal.

So, while exact statistics of body language are different with different situations, people typically agree that communication is not just verbal, and that unspoken communication is important and crucial for the way we interact and understand one another as humans. This is especially true in emotionally charged conversations.

Nonverbal signals, cues, and meanings are especially important when we are very first meeting someone. Our opinions of a new person are formed within the first few seconds of interaction, and this primal, instinctive judgment is based a lot more on what we feel and observe about the person, rather than which words they choose to use.

Are First Impressions Really the Most Important?

You may be able to recall situations where you had a strong opinion of someone before you even heard them speak, and this is not uncommon. It is our human instincts at work, built upon thousands of years of evolution. As a consequence of this function, body language is extremely influential in the forming of our first impressions of a new person we are meeting. The effect goes both ways:

When we first encounter and meet a new person, the language of their body plays a large role in our first impression of them, on both subconscious and conscious levels. Much of this reaction is instinctual and beyond the control of our conscious minds.

Likewise, when another person meets us initially, they are already forming their first impression and how they feel about us mainly from our non-verbal cues and the language of our body.

More Reasons to Become Aware of this Language:

This mutual exchange of body language signals will continue on throughout our relationships and interactions with other people, which means the subject is highly important to become aware of. This language is always being exchanged and traded between us, whether we are aware of it or not, and many times, it is occurring on a level that is below our conscious minds. Keep in mind that while you are reading and interpreting another person's unspoken cues (both consciously and subconsciously), they are doing the same to you.

Individuals who have the most awareness consciously of reading the non-verbal language of others usually have a distinct advantage over people who only notice what they see on the surface. The good news is, you can get better at this and transform your life and relationships. You will change your own consciousness of this non-verbal language from the subconscious to the conscious awareness by studying and reading about the subject, then practicing your new findings with yourself and other people you interact with.

Here are some Specific Areas to Begin Thinking about and Focusing On:

Facial Expressions:

This area is integral when it comes to expressing feelings non-verbally. Motions of the cheeks, lips, eyebrows, eyes, and even nose combine to form and convey a myriad of expressions. Studies have shown that expressions of the face and bod language go hand-in-hand when it comes to interpreting feelings.

Face and Body Expressions in Experiments: Experiments in behavioral psychology have proven that recognizing facial expressions can be heavily influenced by what we perceive as expressions of the body. What this means is that our brains process other people's bodily and facial expressions at the same time. Individuals tested in experiments on the subject showed accurate judgment for reading emotions based on expressions of the face.

This can be traced back to the fact that the face and body are typically viewed together in natural settings and that signals for feelings coming from both the body and the face are completely integrated and smooth.

Postures of the Body:
We can detect the emotions of other people through the postures of their body. Studies have proven that body posture is recognized more accurately when a feeling can be compared with another emotion or a neutral feeling.

An Angry vs. Fearful Posture: To take an example, an individual who is angry would typically exhibit dominance over another person, and their posture would give off tendencies of approach. If you compared this to someone experiencing a feeling of fear, they would typically come across as submissive and weak, making their posture display tendencies of avoidance, a distinct opposite to the former posture of an angry individual.

What Sitting Postures can Indicate: People sitting all the way to the back of their chair and leaning with their body forward, nodding their head in response to the conversation can imply that they are relaxed, open, and in a position for listening.

Opposite of this, an individual who has their legs and or arms in a crossed position while kicking their foot slightly shows that they are not emotionally involved in the conversation and are likely feeling a bit restless or impatient.

What Standing Postures can Indicate: In a discussion which involves standing people, an individual stands with their arms and feet both pointing toward the person doing the talking, which suggests that they are interested and attentive to what the speaker is saying.

On the flip side of this, a tiny difference in this stance could signal a lot more than it seems. If this same individual has one of their legs crossed and puts the balance of their whole body onto just one leg, this could be conveying an attitude of casualness.

Expansive and Open Posturing: Nonverbal posturing that is both expansive and open can also play a role in the levels of cortisol and testosterone in the system, both of which have significant effects on the behavior of individuals.

Bodily Gestures:
This section can be defined as motions that are made with parts of the body, such as the head, fingers, legs, arms, and hands. These movements can be either involuntary or voluntary.

Gestures of the Arms: Gestures of the arms can be translated in many different ways. While engaged in a discussion, one may sit or stand with their arms folded, which generally indicates that they are not in a very welcoming state of mind. This could signal that the person's mind is closed and that they are not very willing to listen to another person's point of view.

Another telling gesture of the arms is when someone crosses one of their arms over their other arm. This stance can indicate a feeling of inferiority, insecurities, or a lack of self-confidence.

Gestures of the Hands: When someone uses a lot of hand gestures, this typically indicates that they are in a good state of mind. If the person speaking has their hands in an relaxed position, this will show self-assurance and high confidence levels.

If the person has their hands clenched, it may mean that they are feeling angry or under stress. If they are fidgeting their hands a lot or wringing them, this means that they are feeling anxious or nervous.

Gestures of the Fingers: These gestures are used commonly as a way of exemplifying spoken words, along with denoting the individual's state of mind. In some societies, using your first finger to point is considered unacceptable. In other cultures, pointing directly at someone with the index finger can be considered an aggressive gesture.

Most of us are familiar with the gesture of "thumbs up" which signals something good. However, in other countries, this can be considered very rude and offensive, the equivalent of holding up a middle finger in the USA.

Handshakes in Communication:

We are all familiar with handshakes, the rituals used for greeting, meeting, offering congratulations to others, and more. These rituals can be a good indicator of the confidence or emotion level in the person you are shaking hands with.

Handshake Types: Research has shown that there are several styles of handshake, including the finger squeezing shake, the bone crushing handshake (when someone has too strong of a grip), the limp shake (which involves a weak shake), and more.

Differences in Meanings from Culture to Culture: In the United States, this form of greeting is appropriate and normal for women and men to engage in together. However, in some Islamic countries, men are not allowed to shake hands with or even touch females. In some Hindu societies, men are not allowed to shake hands with females and instead must perform greetings by enacting a praying gesture.

Other Physical Motions in Body Language:

Apart from the familiar methods for discerning body language outlined above, there are some other less obvious ways to read those around you. If you notice someone covering their mouth, for example, they may be experiencing the urge to suppress feelings or be feeling uncertain. This can also signal that the individual is deep in thought and isn't sure what they should say next in conversation.

What you put forth through your nonverbal signals and body language will affect the way others perceive you, how much they respect and like you as a person, and how much trust (if any) they have in you. A lot of people are constantly sending negative or confusing body language signals without being aware of it. Unfortunately for them, both trust and connection can suffer as a result of being unaware.

Body Language is about more than the way we Move:

Nonverbal motions of the body can involve a lot more than just gestures, arm motions, or finger movements. This area can potentially cover the following and more:

How We Hold ourselves: This can involve anything from posture, to the way we cross or don't cross our limbs, to how much space we take up when we are sitting or standing.

How Close we get to Others: The space we place between our own bodies and those of other people have a lot to do with our body language.

The Movement and Focus of our Eyes: The way we focus our eyes, how often we blink, and where we look while speaking or not speaking all play a role in our overall body language and nonverbal communication.

The Way we touch Others and Ourselves: Some people are comfortable touching the arm of the person they are speaking to, or have a tendency to rub their own arm while speaking. All of this plays a role in unspoken language.

How we Hold or Connect with Foreign Objects: The way we hold our bodies in relation to other things, like cigarettes, eye glasses, pens, or clothes, all play a role in how we communicate nonverbally.

Our Perspiration and Heartbeat: Other physical actions which may be less noticeable can also play a part in the language of our bodies.

What is not Considered a Part of Body Language?

There are some areas also which some consider separate from body language, like pauses in speech, volume of the voice, and pitch variations. A lot can happen in these areas which could be missed if we only think about verbal communication and the typical, limited definitions of nonverbal communication and body language.

The type or tone of voice used and other sound signals are not always considered to be a part of nonverbal body language because they are verbal instead of visual or physical. In the same vein, heartbeat and breathing are often excluded from official definitions of nonverbal communication, but play a role in body language anyway.

Why you should Pay Attention to these Signals Anyway:

Regardless of that, the way a person uses their voice is a highly significant and often subconscious part of the way they communicate, and can lend a lot of insight to their underlying emotions and thoughts. A person's heartbeat and the way they breathe can also tell us a lot about what they are truly thinking and feeling. For these reasons, it's smart to consider these factors along with nonverbal communication and body language.

How Eyes Contribute to Understanding and Assessment between People:

This is quite obvious, but the eyes are an important aspect of nonverbal communication. The way we react to the eyes of other people, for example their expression, focus, and movements, and their reactions to ours, play a huge role in the way we assess each other mutually. It also greatly contributes to our understanding of each other both on conscious and unconscious levels.

Using no spoken words, a lot of emotion can be expressed in just one look. The familiar event, depicted in countless works of fiction, of two people meeting each other's glace from across a room is not only a fancy romantic idea; it's based on hard science involving the power of body language communication between humans.

The Evolution of the Language and How to Use it:

The effects listed above, and other examples given in this book, have been a real part of what it means to be a human for countless centuries. Our body and reactions to each other have been developing so long that they have reached a degree that is clever beyond our own conscious scope of comprehension.

Although most of us may take this for granted or even ignore the phenomena surrounding it, we can all learn a great deal about how to recognize this if we only focus and try. Here are some ways to become more aware of this silent language:

By Feeling Interactions instead of Listening: It's easy to get caught up on words when interacting with other people, but much wisdom can be gleaned from learning how to zone in on the signals beyond speech. This involves tapping into the more intuitive parts of our minds during conversation.

By Keeping the Feeling in Mind while Talking: One way to make sure your true thoughts and emotions are coming through while you interact is to fully feel and embody the thought or feeling you wish to convey. This is a great way to become a more effective communicator and take control of your own body language.

By Watching Movies with the Volume Off: Though it may sound strange, this is a good way to get better at reading emotions free from verbal distraction. Next time you are watching a movie or show, mute the television and see how accurately you can guess the person on screen's feelings. You can then re-watch the episode or movie to gauge how accurate your assessments were.

The way we interpret this soundless language, especially expressions of the eyes and face, is embedded in us instinctively, and with just a little bit of conscious awareness, we can become more aware of the signals constantly being traded amongst us. This includes both the signals we are transmitting and the ones we observe in those around us. Practicing this art form will give us a great advantage in many aspects of life, on a personal and professional level.

Learning about this Helps us Understand Ourselves and Develop Self Control:

A lot of people have trouble controlling themselves or being understood. This has a lot to do with being out of touch with their own signals and the way they are understood by others. The more we make an effort to understanding the unspoken meanings in the words and actions of others, the more we can learn about those same things within us.

Once we begin to better understand unspoken communication, we will improve and refine what our own bodies are constantly telling others about us. This change will create a positive personal momentum in how we perform, how we feel day to day, and the things we are capable of achieving. It also helps us to have a stronger influence over other people.

Chapter 3: Evolution and Nature

Unspoken communication is undeniable a part of the evolution of our species, but the question comes up which qualities are inherited and which are developed throughout life. This is a question that is posed with many aspects of human behavior and existence and an important part of figuring out what body language means to you.

The Nature vs. Nurture Aspect of Body Language:

Which parts of this unspoken language come from genetics, and which parts have been conditioned into us? We may never know for sure, and there are countless opinions that differ on the subject. This debate stretches back many years and has been continued up until our present day, complete with scientific research that proves nature being responsible for our body language, and others proving that nurture has more to do with it.

This question becomes even more complicated when we stop to consider the innate ability in humans to learn how to perform and read nonverbal cues. The best answer we can find to the question, then, is that both nature and nurture are responsible. Body language comes partially from what we are born with (nature), especially in specific ways, but also comes from the way we are taught and conditioned to be (nurture). While some nonverbal communication styles are definitely inherited through our genes and expressed the same way by all individuals, other aspects of this language are definitely not.

The recognition of and use of specific fundamental expressions of the face are considered now to be standard for all people. This means that they are genetically decided, consistent, and the same for all people no matter where they are born or live. However, the recognition and use of less obvious and established physical motions (like the winking of the eyes or movements of the hands) and the way people handle their personal space, are considered to be conditioned.

This means that the way people engage in these motions has more to do with their environmental influences than the tendencies they are born with. These expressions depend heavily on culture and groups of society and differ widely from place to place and person to person.

There are certain variations of speech along with voice intonation patterns that go under the category of learned and dependent upon environment. This only applies, however, if you are considering body language as everything that is outside of verbal communication methods.

As a result of these findings, we can be sure that nonverbal communication (the subconscious and conscious receiving and sending of body language motions, in particular), is partially genetically determined and partially taught to us. Therefore, it is both nature and nurture. This can be important to consider for anyone who wants to get a full grasp of what this science truly means and how to use it for improving their lives.

The More Confusing Side of Nonverbal Communication:

The perspectives evolutionarily on the subject of body language are as numerous as they are intriguing in regards to the purpose of this language and the way it's used. Some even exploit this knowledge, which increases the need to become aware of nonverbal cues and what they mean.

Many humans have a habit of lying, pretending, and manipulating. Some even say that it's the nature of people to act this way, though some people don't do it often. For countless reasons individuals do have a tendency to frequently and intentionally hide their real thoughts and emotions. We get used to expecting this from others, so as a result, we do our best to imagine what the other person we are speaking with is thinking about inside. This urge to truly understanding what is behind our social masks gets more intense depending on how important the relationship is.

More Benefits to this Evolutionary Function:
Unspoken and nonverbal language can help us to guard against and manage these urges, especially when it comes to dating or flirting. Knowing how to read this language can also aid people with communication and fixing issues in relationships when speech and conscious actions fail to complete the task.

This language of our bodies has developed despite the intelligence of our conscious mind and our own human awareness and can help to protect us, connect us to similar minds, and even take fundamental care of us. This happens whether we are aware of it or not, but becoming more aware of it (in both ourselves and others) is the best way to wield this power with the results we wish for.

Body Language in Human History:
The relevance of unspoken language in management, personal relations, and general communication has become a mainstream science and interest within recent years. Despite the widespread interest in the phenomenon being relatively new, we have been relying on these signals using our instincts for countless centuries.

We can look to early necessities for the interpretation of body language to poker players from the Wild West in America. Those who won the game had to be highly skilled at handling a six-shooter and also with being aware of their own nonverbal signals and the signals of the people they played with. In even earlier history, the leaders of tribes and explorers needed to have knowledge of how to read the unspoken signals of potential enemies which gave them the ability of knowing who to trust and who to attack or defend against.

Stretching even further back is our ancestors of the cavemen era who definitely had a necessity of accurately reading the unspoken signals of others, due to the fact that spoken language didn't exist yet, that we are aware of. Our ancient ancestors also had to learn how to interpret the movements and unspoken language of animals, and animals had to learn to read us. Humans obviously had the advantage in this respect.

Horse riders, shepherds, and trainers of animals have been highly skilled with reading the body language of animals and still are today. Knowing how to read nonverbal cues and body language, including thoughts and feelings, is encoded in our genes. If we didn't have this innate ability, it's doubtful that our species would have survived up until the present day.

Differences in Men and Women with Reading Body Language:

When it comes to body language interpretation, women have the upper-hand at perceiving and interpreting than men. This could be due to evolutionary reasons, since women had to develop strong skills of reading body language to make up for being more vulnerable physically to men. This extended to protecting their own offspring, which necessitated having high perception for reading signals of dangerous people. Women are not quite as vulnerable physically in present day, yet their capabilities for reading body language still outdo those of males, typically. This means that females can more effectively use body language to receive and send signals than males can.

Women, on average, are more sensitive empathetically than men are, which tends to go hand in hand with capabilities for body language awareness. Apart from other differences between the genders, males and females with high empathetic skills are much better at reading the body language signs of other people.

Chapter 4: Factors that Affect Interpretation

Nonverbal communication is interpreted on an instinctual level by all humans to a certain degree, but this topic is infinitely more complex than just that. This isn't surprising when you stop to consider that the average body can produce up to 700,000 unique motions. Since there is a high potential for confusion when reading other people's nonverbal signals, here are some things to consider when trying to interpret someone's body language:

The Context of the Situation:
This language is highly affected by the context of a situation, meaning that nonverbal cues in one scenario may mean something completely different in a different one. Here are some examples:

If someone scratches their nose, it's often assumed that this is a sign of lying. However, someone may have a genuine itch.

If someone is crossing their arms, we usually assume they are feeling defensive, but they may just be keeping warm.

If someone rubs their eyes, they might actually be relieving some form of irritation, instead of being upset or disbelieving.

Whether you have Enough Evidence or Samples:
One signal alone for body language is not as reliable as multiple signals in conjunction. Groups of signals can give a much clearer indication of true meaning or feelings than just a couple of signals on their own. When trying to read body language, you should:

Avoid looking too far into signals on their own.

Search for multiple signals which, in combination, give support to a genuine and reliable conclusion.

Avoid drawing conclusions from signals that seem mixed or signal opposite things.

Ethnicity and Culture:
Some body language symbols are the same universally, like frowning and smiling, but others are only relevant to certain ethnic groups or cultures. Being aware of differences in body language for differing cultures is becoming even more important since our modern day is becoming increasingly mixed.

Preferences for personal space (the amount of space between people that is comfortable for both parties) varies widely between individuals from differing cultures.

Gender and Age Plays a Role in how Body Language is Interpreted:
A lot of signals for unspoken body language are highly relative and differ depending on the person's characteristics or qualities. One person's gesture in a particular scenario can have a lot more or a lot less meaning when compared with a similar motion used by someone else in another scenario. Here are some examples of how different people may display differing body language signals:

Younger males tend to be less inhibited, possess a lot of natural energy, and as a result partake in more exaggerated gestures.

Elder females, in comparison, tend to have less energy and use less pronounced gestures and postures.

So when you are attempting to assess someone's nonverbal signals, particularly how strong the meanings behind them are, you should keep in mind that these things are often relative and depend on who you are observing.

Deception or Pretense:
You will undoubtedly come across people who control their movements artificially to create a false impression for a specific

purpose. Some signals that can be easily faked are:

Making eye contact directly.

A firmly confident handshake.

These signals can be pretended pretty easily, but it's usually only for short periods of time. It is possible, however, to be consistent with faking these signals. Although you can fake such signals, it's impossible for an individual to always suppress or control their body language signs. This, among others, is a good factor to consider when analyzing lone signals of body language, along with looking for as many signs as you can. You can look for the following if you suspect fake signals:

Contracting pupils.

Lifting of the eyebrows.

Twitching of someone's mouth.

These micro-gestures can be valuable for discerning someone's real motive that lies beneath the potentially fake signals they may be putting forth. Since these motions are typically so small, hard to identify, and subconsciously enacted, they cannot be controlled, which makes them highly useful in observing others.

Signals for Insecurity, Nervousness, or Boredom:

Some nonverbal cues signal negative emotions like insecurity, anxiety, disinterest, or boredom. It can be tempting to view such signals and jump to conclusions that a person has a weakness. You should, however, consider the situation before jumping to any such conclusion, especially if you are in a professional setting.

Many times, it is the particular situation, instead of the individual, that is causing the signals to appear. Here are some samples of situations that could be producing negative signals and emotions in people who are otherwise confident and strong:

Stress unrelated to the situation at hand.

Too much new learning or knowledge at once.

Exhaustion or general tiredness.

Extreme cold or heat.

Being tired or hungry.

Disability or sickness.

Being under the influence of alcohol or drugs.

Change, a new situation, or unfamiliarity.

When Analyzing Someone's Signals, Ask Yourself:

What conditions could be playing a role in the condition or mood of the person I am observing?

What factors could be having an effect on my hastiness to assume things about the person?

It's very important not to rush conclusions, especially ones that reflect negatively on the person being observed, when you are analyzing someone's body language.

Chapter 5: Translating Body Language

When you are observing someone's nonverbal signals into meanings and feelings, keep in mind that one isolated sign alone does not necessarily mean something in particular. Groups of signs are more reliable for deciphering someone's internal state. This book is intended to provide general guidance, rather than an objective way to judge others. Body language is only one of many different indications of motive, meaning, or mood of individuals.

Things to Keep in Mind about Reading Body Language:

This is a new and inexact science, which should be kept in mind when employing it.

No sign alone is enough to be a reliable or objective indication of an internal feeling or state of mind.

Truly understanding nonverbal communication has to do with interpreting multiple signals which are consistent with one another, to indicate or support a specific assumption or belief.

Translation for Nonverbal Signs:

The Eyes:

The eyes are a special and possibly most telling aspect of all body language cues we receive and transmit to other people. All of us can read the eyes of other people without always being aware of why or how, and this quality seems to be something we are born with. Even looking at someone from very far away, we are able to tell when that person is making eye contact with us.

Quite amazingly, we are able to decipher whether someone is focusing on us, can see quite simply the difference between a blank stare, a focused look, a secret look or an awkward and uncomfortable glance. Whether or not we can describe these looks with words or not, we recognize them instantly and are aware of their meanings. Then there are the eyelids to consider, how flexible our eyes are with closing and widening, and the ability of our pupils to contract or expand. When thinking about all of these factors, perhaps it isn't so surprising that we have come to communicate so effectively using just our eyes. (The following applies to the left or right of the individual producing the signs and going through the motions).

Eyes Looking Right: When someone's eyes are looking to the right, it signals that their brain is creating or imagining something. This is because the right side of the brain handles feelings and creativity. If someone is looking to the right when they are relaying facts, it could mean that they are lying. However, it does not necessarily mean that they are lying. It could, instead, signal that they are speculating, speaking hypothetically, or producing a guess.

Eyes Looking Left: When someone's eyes are looking to the left, it typically means that they are remembering or recalling something and being truthful about what they are saying. The left side of the brain handles memories and facts.

The Mouth:

The human mouth is involved in a high number of nonverbal signals, which may not come as a surprise since it has so many functions. The mouth is responsible for verbal communication, obviously, but also feeding of infants, which is psychologically connected to us later in life by emotions of sex, love, and perceived security or lack thereof. The mouth is an important part of body language because:

A person's mouth can be obscured or touched by their own fingers or hands and has a high amount of flexibility, making it an important and expressive portion of the face.

The mouth plays a large role in the expressions of the face. It also possesses a larger variety of moving portions than some of the other parts of the body, which provides a higher potential of variance for different signals.

The ears and nose can only be involved in body language by the fingers or hands, but a person's mouth can act and be observed on its own.

A huge part of nonverbal communication is smiling. If a smile is real, it is symmetrical and affects the eyes as well, but if a smile is fake, it only involves the mouth.

The Head in Nonverbal Communication:
Our heads are significant parts of the body for nonverbal communication. Our heads tend to determine the direction of our bodies and lead our motions, but this central area is also vulnerable and vital, housing our brain. This means that this part of our bodies is used very often in displaying approval or disapproval and also in the body language of self-protection or defensiveness.

Your head, because of a neck structure that is highly flexible, can move forward, turn sideways, draw back, tilt backwards, and tilt forward. Each of those motions has a meaning, which can be understood when thought of in conjunction with other signals of body language. Here are some other reasons why the head is an important aspect of body language and worth paying attention to:

It possesses a face, nose, ears, eyes, and hair, giving it a more complicated and highly visible effect on the muscles. More so than any other part of a human body.

Our heads are always sending messages, subconsciously and consciously, especially when used in combination with our hands, making it busy and dynamic in nonverbal communication.

Our faces, along with the hands, are the most effective at transmitting body language signs.

The Hands:

The body language of our hands is wide and varied, because these are very expressive body parts which often are interacting with our other body parts, forming signals all the time. These parts have more nerves connecting with the brain than all other parts of the body. Hands are very flexible and expressive parts, so it makes sense that they would be used so often to communicate intentional, conscious gestures, and also to perform a large amount of hidden motions which hint at hidden thoughts and feelings going on inside of us. An ear or a nose on its own can't do much to signal emotions, but if you add a finger or a hand to the mix, the possibilities increase and are likely signaling some type of body language communication. Here are what hands are typically used for in body language:

To Illustrate: Hands can be used to shape things in the air, draw pictures, hint at the size of something, and mime activities, such as a telephone call.

To Create of Increase Emphasis: Motions of the hands can provide extra emphasis to speech using chopping motions, jabbing, or pointing.

To Act out Signals: Some examples of this are the gesture of thumbs up, they okay symbol, or even insulting signals.

To Greet or Depart from Others: Many of us wave to say hello to each other and wave again when we are leaving.

Unconscious Movements: Aside from the conscious movements above, more can be inferred by signals acted out with the hands that are not as conscious. These can include the way someone interacts with other body parts, cigarettes, or pens for example. These unspoken motions can mean anything from expectation, to deceit, to doubt, to an open minded state of being.

Experts on body language are usually in agreement about the fact that hands are the most expressive part used in nonverbal communication, apart from the face. A lot of information can be gained from studying the movements of a person's hands, especially when observed in combination with other body language symbols, like posture, expressions, or personal space.

Chapter 6: How Meditation Helps with Body Language

Meditation makes you more aware of everything, including your own non-verbal signals and the signals of those around you. In addition to this, meditation is a useful practice for many other areas of life. What meditation does is helps you become more aware of your mental patterns by helping you see your thought patterns as separate. This means that you are less likely to be distracted by the turbulence of your mind, which will heighten your awareness of the way you are coming across to people and also in their hidden signals and body language.

Meditation will help you with Body Language by:

Quieting your mind and bringing you closer to your own inner-voice and intuition, which is useful in nonverbal communication.

Helping you read the cues of those you interact with. Their signals will become more clear to your mind, which will be less cluttered and noisy.

Increasing your confidence in yourself, making you more self-assured and aware of the signals you put out to others.

Increasing your confidence in interpreting the hidden signals of communication from conversation with others.

All of these benefits, and more, will become available to you when you establish a regular meditation practice. Now, let's get down to some ways to start benefiting from this wonderful and invaluable activity.

Different Types of Meditation and How to do them:

There are countless types of meditation you can try and different types work for different people. Here are a few meditation exercises you can test out to see which works best for you:

The Sitting Meditation: Perhaps the most well-known and standard form, the sitting meditation involves closing your eyes and staying still for a set period of time. You can begin this exercise by sitting on a cushion cross-legged, on a straight backed chair with your feet on the floor, or kneeling. What matters most is that you find a position that is comfortable for you.

Now you will sit still and attempt to notice each thought that crosses your mind. The goal here is not to stop thinking, as many mistakenly believe, but to become aware of the tangent of thoughts in your head that often flies by unnoticed. You can start by setting your timer to short periods of time, such as five minutes, and work your way up to more with every few successions.

The Walking Meditation: For beginners, this may be a more suitable choice. The walking meditation involves walking outside in nature and attempting to draw your attention inward, listening to your thoughts or focusing on your breathing. Many people find this easier than the sitting meditation, since you are engaged in an activity and getting your body moving.

This will help you with body language because you can start to become more familiar with the motions of your own body, the way you carry yourself, and other idiosyncrasies you may never have paid attention to before.

The Candle Flame Meditation: This meditation involves lighting a candle and gazing at it for a set period of time. Fire has always captivated the human spirit, and it's easy to get absorbed in a flame in front of your eyes. Set a timer on your watch or phone and try to sit and stare at the flame, emptying your mind of thoughts. You can then start to focus on your breath until you are in a calm state of being and allow your mind to empty until you can easily become aware of each thought that passes through your mind.

Each of these recommended meditations will be more effective if they are practiced on a regular basis and supplemented with journal entries after each session. The key to becoming more self-aware and, as a consequence, more aware of those around us, is to first become aware of what our own minds are like. We live in constant distraction, absorbed in our minds, every day without realizing it. To become better at reading others and communicating effectively, we must become more mindful, and meditation is the first step.

Conclusion

Thank you again for Buying this book!

I hope this book was able to help you to understand how much of our communication, as humans, has nothing to do with words. We are communicating constantly, whether we realize it or not, and becoming aware of this will help us to not only understand others better, but also to express ourselves more effectively.

The next step is to use the information you gained from this book to become a better communicator both with interpretation and putting messages across.

Thank you and good luck!

www.ingramcontent.com/pod-product-compliance
Lightning Source LLC
Chambersburg PA
CBHW071152280526
45787CB00003B/1495